ISO 9001:2000 STANDARD Paraphrased:

A Quick Resource for Getting Started

Robert W. Peach
Dr. Lawrence A. Wilson

Based on ANSI/ISO/ASQ Q9001-2000
Quality Management Systems – Requirements
(Clauses 4 through 8)

ISO 9001:2000 Standard Paraphrased:
A Quick Resource for Getting Started

©2001 by GOAL/QPC. All rights reserved.

Reproduction of any part of this publication without the written permission of GOAL/QPC is prohibited.

ANSI/ISO/ASQ Q9001-2000 standard used with permission of the American Society for Quality.

Robert W. Peach
Dr. Lawrence A. Wilson

Editor: Michael Clark
Cover and book design: Michele Kierstead

GOAL/QPC
2 Manor Parkway, Salem, NH 03079-2841
Toll free: 800-643-4316
Phone: 603-893-1944
Fax: 603-870-9122
E-mail: service@goalqpc.com
Web site: www.goalqpc.com

Printed in the United States of America

10 9 8 7 6 5 4 3 2 1

ISBN 1-57681-035-6

Notes on Paraphrasing of ISO 9001:2000

This booklet contains a detailed paraphrasing of:

- ISO 9001:2000 Quality Management System Standard, Clauses 4–8

Clause 1: Scope, Clause 2: Normative Reference, and Clause 3: Terms and Definitions contain introductory topics and have not been paraphrased in this booklet.

Contents

Authors' Note vi

Clause 4: Quality management system 1

Clause 5: Management responsibility 5

Clause 6: Resource management 9

Clause 7: Product realization 11

Clause 8: Measurement, analysis and improvement 20

Definitions 25

About the Authors 30

How to Order ISO 9000 Documents 32

Authors' Note

There has been an increasingly wide acceptance of the ISO 9001 Quality Management System Requirements standard. However, individuals and teams have often experienced difficulty in mastering the required technical content, which has contributed to false starts, blind alleys, and delays that might otherwise have been avoided.

Because we are concerned about helping users of the standards attain the highest possible level of understanding, we asked ourselves what we could do to help. Our answer was to create a concise booklet that paraphrases the actual content of the document; presents key information in brief, clear, understandable language; and is fully consistent with the meaning and intent of the standard.

We believe this paraphrasing of the standard/requirements can help teams to quickly understand the nature and extent of their tasks and provide very clear statements of what must be accomplished for certification and registration.

Every effort has been made not to change the meaning of the basic document. For actual phrasing, please refer to the original document. ISO 9000 paraphrasing is based on the U.S. edition of the international standard ANSI/ISO/ASQ Q9001-2000, which is identical to the international version. For information on how to obtain copies of ISO 9001:2000 (ANSI/ISO/ASQ Q9001-2000), see page 32.

A major change in ISO 9001:2000 from the previous version is that ISO 9001, 9002, and 9003 have been combined into ISO 9001. See clause 1.2 in the standard for rules for exclusions from specific requirements of clause 7, for organizations where this may apply.

<u>Underlined words</u> identify statements of higher requirements compared to ISO 9001:1994, or wording that may be interpreted by users to be a statement of higher requirements. Numbering of clauses and sub-clauses exactly follows ISO 9001:2000. Where paraphrased wording takes the form of a list, entries are identified with a bullet.

When paired with GOAL/QPC's pocket guide, *The Memory Jogger™ 9000/2000*, this booklet provides very clear directions on how to create a robust quality system.

Robert W. Peach

Dr. Lawrence A. Wilson

ISO 9001:2000 Quality Management System Standard Paraphrased

4 Quality management system

4.1 General requirements

Establish a Quality Management System (QMS) that conforms to ISO 9001 and is:

- Documented
- Implemented
- Maintained
- <u>Continually improving effectiveness</u>

To implement the quality system processes:

a. Identify and manage those processes

b. Determine process:
- Sequence
- Interaction

c. Determine criteria and methods to ensure:
- Process operation
- Process control

d. Provide needed resources and information to operate and monitor these processes

e. To attain planned results and improvements:
- Measure
- Monitor
- Analyze

f. Take action to achieve results and to continually improve

<u>The QMS is to consider outsourced processes affecting quality.</u>

Note: QMS processes managed to conform to ISO 9001 should include:

- Management responsibility (clause 5)
- Resource management (clause 6)
- Product realization (clause 7)
- Measurement (clause 8)

4.2 Documentation requirements

4.2.1 General

QMS documents are to include:

a. Quality policy and quality objectives
b. Quality manual
c. Documented procedures required to implement this standard
d. Optional documents to ensure process:
   - Planning
   - Operation
   - Control
e. Records required by this standard (see 4.2.4)

Note 1: "Documented procedure" means the procedure is:

- Established
- Documented
- Implemented
- Maintained

Note 2: The amount of QMS documentation depends on:
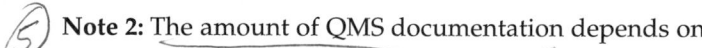

a. Organization size/type
b. Process complexity/interactions
c. Employee competence

Note 3: Documentation can exist in any type of medium, hard copy or electronic.

4.2.2 Quality Manual

Prepare and maintain a quality manual, which includes:

a. The QMS scope, and if there are exclusions:
   - What they are
   - Why they have been made

b. Documented procedures (or references)

c. The interaction between QMS processes

4.2.3 Control of documents

Control those documents where the QMS requires that a documented procedure must be written for this topic:

a. Before being issued, all documents are approved for adequacy.

b. Current documents are:
   - Reviewed
   - Kept updated
   - Re-approved

c. The current version is noted.

d. Current documents are at the place where needed.

e. Documents are:
   - Readable
   - Easily identified
   - Available when needed

f. Documents originating from outside the organization are:
   - Identified
   - Controlled

g. Obsolete documents:
   - Are taken out of circulation
   - Identified if retained, to prevent misuse

4.2.4 Control of records

Maintain and control required records to demonstrate that:
- Requirements are being met
- The QMS is working effectively

The documented procedure for quality records defines:
- Identification
- Legibility
- Storage
- Protection
- Retrieval
- Retention time
- Disposition

5 Management responsibility

5.1 Management commitment

Top management is to be committed to developing, implementing, and improving the quality system by:

a. Making certain everyone understands the importance of meeting the needs of:
   - Customers
   - Regulations

b. Establishing quality policy

c. Establishing objectives

d. Conducting management reviews

e. Providing resources

5.2 Customer focus

Make certain that requirements to satisfy the customers are:

- Defined
- Met (see 7.2.1. and 8.2.1)

5.3 Quality Policy

Make certain the quality policy:

a. Is appropriate for organizational goals

b. Includes commitment to:
   - Meeting requirements
   - Continually improve effectiveness of the QMS

c. Provides for:
   - Establishing
   - Reviewing

   quality objectives

d. Is:
- Communicated to everyone affected
- Understood by everyone affected

e. Is evaluated for continuing suitability

5.4 Planning

5.4.1 Quality objectives

Quality objectives are to be:

- Established for each appropriate organizational function
- Measurable
- Consistent with quality policy

Meeting product requirements is a quality objective (see 7.1a).

5.4.2 Quality management system planning

Top management is to ensure that:
a. QMS processes are planned to meet:
- Requirements of 4.1
- Quality objectives

b. Integrity of the QMS is maintained when changes are made

5.5 Responsibility, authority and communication

5.5.1 Responsibility and authority

Roles and their responsibilities and authorities are to be:
- Defined
- Communicated

5.5.2 Management representative

Designate member of management with defined authority to:
a. Establish, implement, and maintain QMS processes

b. Report on the performance of the QMS, with improvement needs

c. <u>Ensure that customer needs are well known in the organization</u>

Note: Management representatives often interface with outside parties on quality issues.

5.5.3 Internal communication

<u>Make certain that the process exists to communicate the effectiveness of the QMS to all levels and functions.</u>

5.6 Management review

5.6.1 General

- Management is to review the QMS periodically, to:
    - Ensure that it continues to be:
        - Suitable
        - Adequate
        - Effective
    - Consider whether modifications in the QMS, such as policy and objectives, are needed

Management review records are to be maintained (see 4.2.4).

5.6.2 Review <u>input</u>

<u>Review performance related to:</u>

a. Audit results

b. Feedback from customers

c. Performance of the process and conformance of the product

d. Preventive and corrective actions

e. Follow-up from previous reviews

f. Changes affecting the QMS

g. Improvement recommendations

©2001 GOAL/QPC — ISO 9001:2000 Standard Paraphrased — 7

5.6.3 Review output

Management review outputs are to include decisions and actions concerned with:

a. Effectiveness of the QMS
b. Product improvement based on customer needs
c. Needed resources

6 Resource management

6.1 Provision of resources

Identify and provide necessary resources to:

a. Establish, maintain, and improve the effectiveness of the QMS

b. Enhance satisfaction of customers by meeting their requirements

6.2 Human resources

6.2.1 General

Make certain that all personnel with activities affecting quality are appropriately qualified as to:

- Education
- Training
- Skills
- Experience

6.2.2 Competence, awareness and training

The organization is to:

a. Identify competency needs

b. Train to meet these needs or take alternative action

c. Judge the effectiveness of training

d. Make all employees aware of:
   - The importance of their work
   - The impact they have on quality objectives

e. Maintain relevant records for:
   - Education
   - Training
   - Qualification
   - Experience (see 4.2.4)

6.3 Infrastructure

To ensure conformity, necessary facilities are to be:

- Identified
- Provided
- Maintained

including:

a. Buildings, work areas, and facilities

b. Process equipment:
   - Hardware
   - Software

c. Supporting services:
   - Transportation
   - Communication

6.4 Work environment

To achieve product conformance, factors of the work environment (human/physical) should be:

- Determined
- Managed

7   Product realization

7.1   Planning of product realization

Process planning is to be consistent with the QMS (see 4.1).

Process realization planning defines, as necessary:

a. <u>Quality objectives and product requirements</u>

b. Needed:
   - Processes
   - Documentation
   - Resources

   for each product

c. Post-process procedures:
   - Verification
   - <u>Validation</u>
   - Monitoring
   - Inspection and test
   - Acceptance criteria

d. Needed records to demonstrate requirements are met by:
   - Processes
   - Product (see 4.2.4)

The form of planning output is to meet the organization's method of operation.

Note 1: A document on how the QMS applies to a specific:
- Product
- Project, or
- Contract

may be considered as a quality plan.

Note 2: Design and development requirements in 7.3 may be applied to product realization processes.

7.2 Customer-related processes

7.2.1 Determination of requirements related to the product

Identify requirements, including:

a. Customer requirements for

- Delivery
- Post-delivery

b. <u>Unstated, but necessary requirements for specified or intended customer use, where known</u>

c. Statutory and regulatory obligations

d. Any other requirements set by the organization

7.2.2 Review of requirements related to the product

Review all requirements including those from the customer before making a commitment, such as:

- Submitting a tender/order
- Accepting a contract
- Accepting a change in contract

to be sure that:

a. Requirements are defined

b. Changes from initial tender or quotation are resolved

c. Requirements can be met

Record results of reviews and follow-up actions.

Verbal agreements are to be confirmed.

Where requirements change:

- Update necessary documentation
- Notify personnel involved

Note: Where a formal review is not practical (such as Internet sales), review can consist of specific product information available to customers in advertising and catalogs.

7.2.3 Customer communication

Establish customer communication channels related to:

a. Product information

b. Handling:
- Inquiries
- Contracts
- Orders
- Amendments

c. Feedback from customers, including complaints

7.3 Design and development

7.3.1 Design and development planning

Plan and control product design and development activities, including:

a. Stages of design and development

b. Necessary review, verification, and validation

c. Assigning implementation responsibilities

Manage the interfaces between the groups that contribute to design/development to ensure:
- Effective communication
- Clear task assignment responsibilities

Update planning output as progress is made.

7.3.2 Design and development inputs

Define and record necessary inputs for the following product requirements (see 4.2.4):

a. Function and performance

b. Relevant statutory and regulatory requirements

c. Those derived from similar designs

d. Other necessary requirements

Resolved input requirements are to be:
- Complete
- Unambiguous
- Not conflicting

7.3.3 Design and development outputs

Record outputs so that they can be compared to inputs prior to release.

Output must:

a. Meet input requirements

b. Provide purchasing, production, and service information

c. Contain or reference criteria for determining that requirements are met

d. Identify characteristics crucial to safety and correct application

7.3.4 Design and development review

According to plan, as in 7.3.1, review design/development status at suitable stages, systematically, to:

a. Determine the capability to meet requirements

b. Target problems and possible solutions

Include representation of relevant organizations.

Record review findings and subsequent actions (see 4.2.4).

7.3.5 Design and development verification

Conduct verification as planned in 7.3.1, to ensure that output meets input.

Record verification results and follow-up actions (see 4.2.4).

7.3.6   Design and development validation

Validate, to make certain that the product is capable of meeting the intended application, as planned in 7.3.1 and as specified.

Complete validation prior to delivery, where practical.

Record validation results and follow-up actions.

7.3.7   Control of design and development changes

Changes are to be:
- Identified
- Recorded

Before release, changes are to be:
- Reviewed, verified, and validated, as appropriate
- Approved

Define the impact of changes on:
- Parts
- Products already delivered

Record the results and follow-up actions (see 4.2.4).

7.4   Purchasing

7.4.1   Purchasing process

Ensure that purchases meet requirements.

The nature of control depends on the effect on later processes and output.

Evaluate and choose suppliers on their ability to meet requirements.

Define criteria for supplier:
- Selection
- Evaluation
- Re-evaluation

Record evaluations and follow-up actions (see 4.2.4).

7.4.2 Purchasing information

Purchasing information describing what is ordered, is to include, as appropriate:

a. Requirements for approval of:
- Product
- Procedures
- Processes
- Equipment

b. Requirements for qualification of personnel

c. QMS requirements

Make sure the purchasing documents adequately specify requirements prior to release.

7.4.3 Verification of purchased product

Verify purchased product as necessary.

When the organization verifies product at the supplier's site, purchasing documents are to describe:
- Plans for verification
- How the product is to be released

7.5 Production and service provision

7.5.1 Control of production and service provision

Controlled conditions are required for production and service provisions through:

a. Information describing necessary characteristics

b. Work instructions where needed

c. Suitable equipment

d. Use of suitable monitoring and measuring devices

e. Implementation of monitoring and measurement

f. Defined processes for release, delivery, and activities after delivery

7.5.2 Validation of processes for production and service provision

Validate processes where it may not be possible to verify quality by later checking, including cases where deficiencies are only seen after delivery or usage.

Validate such processes to show their acceptability.

When applicable, the validation plan is to:

a. Review and approve processes to defined criteria

b. Use qualified equipment and personnel

c. Use specific methods and procedures

d. Determine need for records (see 4.2.4)

e. Re-validate

7.5.3 Identification and traceability

Identify the product, as necessary, during product realization.

Identify status of monitoring and measurement requirements.

Where required, control and record unique traceability identification of product (see 4.2.4).

Note: Identification and traceability are maintained by configuration management in some industries.

7.5.4 Customer property

Customer property is to be handled with care, ensuring:

- Identification
- Verification
- Protection
- Safeguarding

Report to customers a record (see 4.2.4) of any product that is:

- Lost
- Damaged
- Unsuitable for use

Note: Includes intellectual property

7.5.5 Preservation of product

Make certain that, during internal processing and delivery, conformance with customer requirements is not altered by:

- Identification
- Handling
- Packaging
- Storage
- Preservation

This also applies to product parts.

7.6 Control of monitoring and measuring devices

To ensure product conformity, define:

- Needed monitoring and measurements
- Required monitoring and measuring devices (see 7.2.1)

Make certain that such devices are used properly, ensuring that capability meets requirements.

Where needed to ensure valid results:

a. Calibrate such devices:
   - At prescribed intervals, or prior to use
   - To certified equipment, with valid relationship to international or national standards. (If not, document the basis actually used.)

b. Adjust or readjust as needed

c. Identify to ensure calibration status

d. Protect the devices from being adjusted in a way that would cause calibration settings to be incorrect

e. Protect such devices from damage by providing suitable methods of:
   - Handling
   - Maintenance
   - Preservation
   - Storage

Review the validity of previous monitoring and measuring results when equipment is found out of calibration, and take necessary actions.

Maintain calibration and verification records (see 4.2.4).

<u>Prior to initial use, validate monitoring and measurement software.</u>

Note: See ISO 10012 for guidance.

8 Measurement, analysis and improvement

8.1 General

Plan and put into use necessary monitoring and measurement analysis and improvement functions to demonstrate:

a. That the product meets requirements

b. Conformity of the QMS requirements

c. Continual improvement of QMS effectiveness

Identify and use necessary methods, including statistical techniques.

8.2 Monitoring and measurement

8.2.1 Customer satisfaction

Track information on perception of customer satisfaction, as one indicator of QMS performance.

Define how such information will be obtained and used.

8.2.2 Internal audit

Conduct audits at planned intervals to learn if the QMS:

a. Conforms to plan, to this standard, and to QMS requirements (see 7.1)

b. Is in effective operation, and is being maintained

The audit process is based on:

- Status and significance of audit target
- Previous audit results

Define audit:

- Criteria
- Scope
- Frequency
- Methods

Conduct audits with personnel who are objective, impartial, and independent of the activity being audited.

A documented procedure for audits should cover:
- Responsibilities
- Requirements
- Records (see 4.2.4)
- Report of results

With deficiencies found:
- Take timely corrective action
- Verify implementation
- Report verification results (see 8.5.2)

Note: See ISO 10011 series for guidance.

8.2.3 Monitoring and measurement of processes

Monitor and measure QMS processes to meet:
- Customer requirements
- Their intended purpose

Take corrective action, as appropriate, when planned results are not achieved.

8.2.4 Monitoring and measurement of product

Product characteristics are to be measured and monitored at appropriate stages to show that requirements are met (see 7.1).

Document (see 8.2.4):
- Conformance with acceptance criteria
- Authority to release

Unless otherwise customer-approved, do not release and deliver product until required activities have been satisfactorily accomplished.

8.3 Control of nonconforming product

To avoid unintended use, make sure nonconformities are:

- Identified
- Controlled

Define such arrangements in a documented procedure.

Response when nonconforming product is detected may include:

a. Eliminating the nonconformity

b. Authorizing acceptance for use by appropriate authority (where applicable, the customer)

c. Regrading for alternative applications

Maintain records of nonconformities and actions, including concessions.

Re-verify that corrected product conforms to requirements.

If uncovered after delivery, take necessary action.

8.4 Analysis of data

Determine and gather data:

- To measure the effectiveness of the QMS
- To target improvement opportunities
- From monitoring and measuring activities and elsewhere

From these data, provide an analysis of:

a. Customer satisfaction (see 8.2.1)

b. How well requirements of customers are met (see 7.2.1)

c. Characteristics and trends of processes and products looking for ways to identify and prevent potential problems

d. Suppliers

8.5 Improvement

8.5.1 Continual improvement

<u>Continually improve the effectiveness of the QMS by using:</u>
- Quality policy
- Quality objectives
- Audit results
- Data analysis
- Corrective/preventive actions
- Management review

8.5.2 Corrective action

To prevent repeat nonconformities, focus on eliminating causes and take corrective action appropriate to the problem.

A documented procedure for corrective action is to establish requirements for:

a. Identifying nonconformities (includes customer complaints)

b. Determining causes

c. Evaluating actions to avoid recurrence

d. Implementing corrective actions

e. Recording the results (see 4.2.1)

f. Reviewing action taken

8.5.3 Preventive action

<u>Take steps to identify the causes of potential nonconformities</u> and take appropriate preventive action.

A documented procedure for preventive action shall:

a. Identify causes of potential nonconformities

b. Evaluate the need for action to prevent nonconformance

c. Determine and take actions needed

d. Record results (see 4.2.4)

e. Review action taken

Definitions

Definitions identified with a clause number are taken from ANSI/ISO/ASQ Q9000 (reprinted with permission of the American Society for Quality).

Continual improvement is the recurring activity to increase the ability to fulfill requirements (clause 3.2.13).

Corrective action is the action taken to eliminate the cause of a detected nonconformity or other undesirable situation (clause 3.6.5).

Customer is the organization or person that receives a product (clause 3.3.5).

Defect is the non-fulfillment of a requirement related to an intended or specific use. The distinction between the concepts defect and nonconformity is important, as it has legal connotations, particularly those associated with product liability issues. Consequently the term "defect" should be used with extreme caution (clause 3.6.3).

Design and development is a set of processes that transforms requirements into specified characteristics or into the specification of a product process or system. The terms "design" and "development" are sometimes used synonymously and sometimes used to define different stages of the overall design and development process (clause 3.4.4).

Design review is a formal, documented, comprehensive, and systematic examination of the status of a design in order to evaluate the design input requirements against the capability of the design to meet these input requirements, and to identify problems and propose solutions.

Documentation of the quality management system is a systematic and understandable description and transcription of those policies and procedures affecting product and service quality.

Documents, in ISO 9000 usage, are causative and generally consist of permanent documentation describing or defining systems, processes, procedures, and product. Examples include product specifications and quality manuals.

Documented procedure is permanent objective evidence of a defined or specified way to carry out an activity or process.

Effectiveness is the extent to which planned activities are realized and planned results achieved (clause 3.2.14).

Efficiency is the relation between the result achieved and the resources used (clause 3.2.15).

End user is the ultimate consumer of a product or service, which may or may not be the customer.

Infrastructure is the set of facilities, equipment, or services needed for the operation of an organization (clause 3.3.3).

Interested party is the person or group having an interest in the successful performance of an organization, e.g., customers, owners, people in an organization, suppliers, bankers, unions, partners, or society (clause 3.3.7).

Inspection is conformity evaluation by observation and judgement accompanied by measurement, testing, or gauging (clause 3.8.2).

ISO is the International Organization for Standardization, a worldwide federation of national standards bodies formed in 1947. ISO produces standards in all fields except electrical and electronic (which are covered by the International Electrotechnical Commission or IEC).

Management review is the review of the quality system by management to ensure the quality system remains suitable and effective.

Measurement is the process of determining the value of a quantity (clause 3.10.2).

Nonconformity is the non-fulfillment of a requirement (clause 3.6.2). See also **defect**.

Preventive action is the action taken to eliminate the cause of a potential nonconformity or other potentially undesirable situation (clause 3.6.4).

Process is the set of interrelated or interacting activities that transforms inputs into outputs. A process where conformity of the resulting product cannot be readily or economically verified is frequently referred to as a "special process" (clause 3.4.1).

Process approach is the managing of a system of processes within an organization, together with the identification, application, and interactions of these processes.

Process control is the identification of and action on all identified factors affecting process variability, including materials accepted into the process, proper maintenance of equipment, use of statistical process control methods, and degree of adherence to valid work instructions.

Product is the result of a process (clause 3.4.2). There are four generic product categories: services (e.g., transport), software (computer programs), hardware (mechanical parts), and processed materials (lubricants). Many products comprise elements belonging to different generic product categories.

Quality is the degree to which a set of inherent characteristics fulfills requirements (clause 3.1.1).

Quality audit is the systematic, independent, and documented process for obtaining audit evidence and evaluating it objectively to determine the extent to which agreed criteria are fulfilled (clause 3.9.1).

Quality management is the coordinated activities to direct and control an organization with regard to quality. Direction and control with regard to quality generally includes establishment of the quality policy, quality objectives, quality planning, quality control, quality assurance, and quality improvement (clause 3.2.8).

Quality management system is a set of interrelated or interacting processes with regard to quality, accomplished by the management of an organization by establishing policy and objectives, and by achieving those objectives (clause 3.2.1, -2, -3).

Quality manual is the document specifying the quality management system of an organization (clause 3.7.4).

Quality plan is the document specifying which procedures and associated resources shall be applied by whom and when to a specific project, product, process, or contract. Establishing quality plans can be a part of quality planning (clause 3.7.5).

Quality planning is the part of quality management focused on setting quality objectives and specifying necessary operational processes and related resources to fulfill the quality objectives (clause 3.2.9).

Quality policy is the overall intentions and direction of an organization related to quality as formally expressed by top management (clause 3.2.4).

Records are the documents providing current and historical evidence of activities conducted. Electronic data are acceptable as a record. Examples include inspection and test records, records confirming traceability, evidence of verification, or preventive and corrective action (based on clause 3.7.6).

Regulatory requirements are requirements established by governmental agencies or other regulatory bodies (i.e., industry).

Statutory requirements are requirements based on statutory law, as opposed to case law or common law.

Statistical process control is the application of statistical techniques to the control of processes.

Supplier is the organization or person that provides a product (clause 3.3.6).

Top management is the person or group of people who direct and control an organization at the highest level (clause 3.2.7).

Traceability is the ability to trace the history, application, or location of that which is under consideration (clause 3.5.4).

Training is the result of teaching and learning, so as to be fitted, qualified, or proficient in a specific task.

Validation is the confirmation, through the provision of objective evidence, that the requirements for a specific intended use or application have been fulfilled (clause 3.8.5).

Verification is confirmation, through the provision of objective evidence, that specific requirements have been fulfilled (clause 3.8.4).

Work environment is the set of conditions under which work is performed. Conditions include physical, social, psychological, and environmental factors such as temperature, recognition schemes, ergonomics, and atmospheric composition (clause 3.3.4).

About the Authors

Robert W. Peach

Current Positions

- Editor, *The ISO 9000 Handbook*, published by McGraw-Hill, Inc.
- Co-author, *The Memory Jogger™ 9000* and *The Memory Jogger™ 9000/2000*, published by GOAL/QPC
- Principal, Robert Peach and Associates, Inc.

Past Positions

- Quality Assurance Manager, Sears Roebuck and Company
- Project Manager, Malcolm Baldrige National Quality Award Consortium
- Convenor, Working Group that developed ISO 9004-1
- Chair, Registrar Accreditation Board

Education and Recognitions

- BS in Business and Engineering Administration, MIT
- MBA, University of Chicago
- Fellow, American Society for Quality
- Recipient of ASQ Edwards Medal
- Registered Professional Engineer, Quality Engineering

About the Authors

Dr. Lawrence A. Wilson

Current Positions

- President, Lawrence A. Wilson & Associates

- Lead U.S. Delegate to ISO International Working Group that prepared ISO 9001/9004:2000 as a consistent pair of standards

- Author of *Eight-Step Process to Successful ISO 9000 Implementation* and *How to Implement ISO 9000*, Learner First Software, both published by Quality Press

Past Positions

- Director of Product Assurance and Safety, Lockheed Aeronautical Systems Company – Georgia Division

- Convenor of Group for ISO 10013, Quality Manuals

- Chair, Defense Contractor/Aerospace QA Committees

Education and Recognitions

- Ph.D. in Radiation Biophysics, Emory University

- BS/MS in the Sciences, Kent State University

- Registered Professional Engineer, Quality Engineering

How to Order
ISO 9000 Documents

ISO 9000 Standards Resources

United States:
American National Standards Institute
1819 L Street, NW
Suite 600
Washington, DC 20036
Phone: (202) 293-8020   Fax: (202) 293-9287
www.ansi.org

Canada:
CSA International
178 Rexdale Boulevard
Toronto, Ontario
Canada M9W 1R3
Phone: (416) 747-4000   Fax: (416) 747-2475
www.csa-international.org

ANSI/ISO/ASQ Q9001-2000
Quality Management Systems - Requirements

ASQ Quality Press
Customer Service Department
611 E. Wisconsin Avenue
P.O. Box 3005
Milwaukee, WI 53201-3005
Phone: (800) 248-1946   Fax: (414) 272-1734
www.qualitypress.asq.org

How to Order Additional Copies of this Booklet

CALL TOLL FREE
800-643-4316
or 603-893-1944
8:30 AM – 5:00 PM EST

MAIL
GOAL/QPC
2 Manor Parkway
Salem, NH
03079-2841

WEB SITE
www.goalqpc.com

FAX
603-870-9122

E-MAIL
service@goalqpc.com

Price Per Copy

Quantity	Price
1–9	$5.95
10–49	$5.20
50–99	$4.65
100–499	$4.25
500–1999	$4.15

For quantities of 2000 or more, call for a quote.

Sales Tax

Canada   7% of order

Shipping & Handling Charges

Continental US: Orders up to $10 = $2 (U.S. Mail). Orders $10 or more = $4 + 4% of order (guaranteed Ground Delivery). Call for overnight, 2-day & 3-day delivery. **For Alaska, Hawaii, Canada, Puerto Rico, and other countries, please call.**

Payment Methods

We accept payment in U.S. dollars drawn on a U.S. bank by check, money order, credit card, or purchase order. **If you pay by purchase order:** 1) Provide the name and address of the person to be billed, or 2) Send a copy of the P.O. when order is payable by an agency of the federal government.

Order Form

1. Shipping Address (We cannot ship to a P.O. Box)

Name _____

Title _____

Company _____

Address _____ City _____

State _____ Zip _____ Country _____

Phone _____ Fax _____

E-mail _____

2. Quantity & Price

Code	Quantity	Unit Price	Total Price
1200P			

	Tax Canada only	
	Shipping & Handling See previous page	
	Total	

3. Payment Method

❒ Check enclosed (payable to GOAL/QPC) $ _____

❒ VISA ❒ MasterCard ❒ Amex

❒ Diners Club ❒ Discover

Card # _____ Exp. date _____

Signature _____

❒ Purchase order # _____

Bill to _____

Address _____

City _____

State _____ Zip _____ Country _____

4. Request for Other Materials

❒ GOAL/QPC catalog

❒ Information on customization

ISO9001:2000

The Memory Jogger™ 9000/2000

A Pocket Guide to Implementing the ISO 9001 Quality Systems Standard Based on ANSI/ISO/ASQ Q9001-2000

Robert Peach, Bill Peach, and Diane Ritter

"The Memory Jogger™ 9000/2000 is a wonderfully put together document. For someone with knowledge of the 1994 standards, this new Memory Jogger™ is an easy way to be brought up to speed."

Peter Teti, CQE, CQA
United Technologies

Fits in your pocket

- Updated ISO 9001:2000 clause names and structures, paraphrased and organized into easy-to-follow sections
- Examples, notes, pitfalls, and illustrations to foster understanding
- Comparison of ISO 9000:1994 and ISO 9001:2000 clause structures
- Comparison of ISO 9001:2000 to Malcolm Baldrige National Quality Award criteria

Just starting your ISO registration process? Now you can understand and implement ISO 9001:2000 quickly, easily, and effectively. *The Memory Jogger™ 9000/2000* will guide you through the latest modifications to the ISO 9001 standard, with easy-to-follow instructions to prepare for, implement, and maintain ISO registration. This powerful pocket guide provides each employee with a clear understanding of the changes in terminology and clause structure from the 1994 standard, and answers key questions about each employee's role in the registration process. *The Memory Jogger™ 9000/2000* will be a cornerstone for the successful registration and implementation of ISO 9001:2000 in any organization. Measures 3.5" x 5.5". 2000. 180 pages. ISBN 1-57681-032-1.

Code 1065E
$7.95

The Memory Jogger™ II

A Pocket Guide of Tools for Continuous Improvement and Effective Planning

Michael Brassard and Diane Ritter

"GOAL/QPC Memory Joggers™ are invaluable in the day-to-day quest for continuous improvement. They provide clear, concise, easy-to-use guidance in a convenient, portable, package."

Fred C. Herald III
Process Improvement Consultant
NCR Corporation

Fits in your pocket

- Learn how to use the basic Quality Control Tools and the Seven Management & Planning Tools
- Learn how to collect data and formulate solutions
- Streamline inefficient processes
- Manage and plan projects
- Make better, more informed decisions

This pocket guide describes the use of basic tools for making continuous improvements in your organization. Your teams can become more focused and productive, more skilled in identifying and solving critical problems, and more effective in planning for data- and consensus-inspired action plans and results. *The Memory Jogger™ II* uses a case study example to show you how the tools, when used in combination, can become more powerful and effective for solving problems and reaching goals. It includes examples from well-known organizations in a variety of industries that show how real people have used the tools in their workplaces and why these tools are effective, providing clear, step-by-step illustrations that help you construct, understand, and use each tool. Measures 3.5" x 5.5". 1994. 164 pages. ISBN 1-879364-44-1.

Code 1030E
$7.95

Facilitation at a Glance!
Your Pocket Guide to Facilitation

Ingrid Bens

"GOAL/QPC has assembled a unique collection of useful training and 'how-to' materials to address a variety of organizational problems. Over the past decade, many have been shown to have enduring value."

Jack Brown
Director Worldwide Quality Assurance
Procter & Gamble Company

- Understand the role of the facilitator
- Plan facilitation strategies
- Create effective team participation
- Manage conflict
- Manage meetings

As organizations grow increasingly dependent on the interactions of people to get things done, they find team effectiveness directly related to productivity and success. That's why many companies now rely on internal facilitators to help teams become as proficient in process (the way they work together) as they are in content (their subject expertise). Facilitators help teams keep on track, minimize nonproductive behaviors, and reach effective decisions.

Facilitation at a Glance!, co-published by GOAL/QPC and The Association for Quality and Participation (AQP), is a handy pocket guide for facilitators in any business or organization. Packed with useful information, tips, and techniques, *Facilitation at a Glance!* will assist both new and experienced facilitators in their efforts to maximize team effectiveness and achieve increased productivity. Measures 3.5" x 5.5". 1999. 170 pages. ISBN 1-890416-05-3.

Code 1062E
$7.95

The Problem Solving Memory Jogger™
Seven Steps to Improved Processes

GOAL/QPC

"When I am preparing for or engaged in problem-solving, decision-making, or knowledge-based activities, there are no reference materials that I use more frequently than the GOAL/QPC Memory Joggers™."

Kirk Hamsher
Learning Specialist
Abbott Laboratories (Diagnostic Division)

- A proven, standardized, 7-step problem-solving methodology
- Instructions on how to use a variety of data analysis and decision-making tools
- A case study to illustrate the 7-step methodology and use of the tools
- Information on additional tools that can "turbo-charge" the performance of each step in the process
- Clear links to other pocket guides in the Memory Jogger™ series
- Information on advanced problem-solving techniques

The Problem Solving Memory Jogger™ is an easy-to-use pocket guide designed to help teams or individuals use a 7-step method to solve organizational problems. This method includes several data analysis and decision-support tools that enable teams and individuals to clearly describe process-related problems, isolate their root causes, create effective solutions, and standardize process improvements so the problem does not occur again.

The Problem Solving Memory Jogger™ is an indispensable training and performance support resource that will result in improved effectiveness for your problem-solving teams and, ultimately, optimized processes. Measures 3.5" x 5.5". 2000. 156 pages. ISBN 1-57681-031-3.

Code 1070E
$7.95

Project Management Memory Jogger™
A Pocket Guide for Project Teams

Paula Martin and Karen Tate

"Only people who have actually experienced the pain of projects failing and the bliss of difficult projects succeeding could have formulated this little beauty."

Bea Glenn
Organizational Development Consultant
Chiquita Banana International,
Cincinnati, OH

Fits in your pocket

- Allocate scarce resources
- Meet critical deadlines
- Stay within budget limits
- Meet or exceed customer requirements

The *Project Management Memory Jogger*™ is the most cost-effective way to ensure that your project teams achieve high-quality results. It provides every member of your organization with an easy-to-use road map for managing all types of projects. Whether your team is planning the construction of a new facility or implementing a customer feedback system, this pocket guide helps you avoid typical problems and pitfalls and create successful project outcomes every time. It is packed with useful information on everything from project concept to completion.

The method described in the *Project Management Memory Jogger*™ is consistent with industry standard approaches such as PMBOK, with an emphasis on participation, empowerment, individual accountability, and bottom-line project results. It utilizes tools and concepts from continuous process improvement and applies those to making project management something that is accessible to all teams working on projects. Measures 3.5" x 5.5". 1997. 170 pages. ISBN 1-57681-001-1.

Code 1035E
$7.95

The Team Memory Jogger™
A Pocket Guide for Team Members

A GOAL/QPC–Oriel Incorporated Publication

"Both The Team Memory Jogger™ *and* The Memory Jogger™ II *have played an important role in Inco's Ontario Division. We have included these pocket guides with our own training material for a 'Quality Overview' course, and attendees have said they are both instructive and good references for facilitating groups, which they do back in the workplace."*

Bill Dopson
Divisional TQ Coordinator
Inco Limited (Ontario Division)

Fits in your pocket

- Learn how to be an effective team member
- Identify key issues that your teams need to address
- Get work done more efficiently in teams
- Know when and how to end a project
- Manage conflict more effectively

The Team Memory Jogger™ is perfect for every member of your team. Each topic is discussed from the viewpoint of a team member and what one can contribute to the team. This friendly pocket guide is relevant to all kinds of teams; project, process improvement, self-directed or intact work teams, task forces, and so on.

Written in collaboration with Oriel Inc. (formerly Joiner Associates, Inc.), this pocket guide has become a phenomenal hit for one simple reason—it contains teamwork strategies that really work. Since its introduction in 1995, many organizations have incorporated *The Team Memory Jogger*™ as their standard reference in courses on team effectiveness.

The Team Memory Jogger™ goes beyond theory to provide you with practical, nuts-and-bolts action steps on how to be an effective team member. It is a perfect complement to *The Memory Jogger*™ *II*. Measures 3.5" x 5.5". 1995. 164 pages. ISBN 1-879364-51-4.

Code 1050E
$7.95

Notes

Notes